CHOCOLATE
The Consuming Passion

CHOCOLATE

The Consuming Passion
by Sandra Boynton

Boynton

Workman Publishing, New York

Library of Congress Cataloging in Publication Data

Boynton, Sandra.
Chocolate, the consuming passion.

1. Chocolate—Anecdotes. facetiae, satire, etc.
I. Title.

PN6231.C33B69   641.3′374′0207   81-43781
ISBN 0-89480-199-6   AACR2
ISBN 0-89480-197-X (cloth)

Workman Publishing
708 Broadway
New York, New York 10003

Manufactured in Hong Kong

First printing April 1982

15 14 13 12 11 10 9

Photo Credits:
Baker, H. Armstrong Roberts
German, Frederic Lewis
Dwight D. Eisenhower, The Bettmann Archive, Inc.
Foods, The Bettmann Archive, Inc.

Text Permission:
Shell plant production sequence from
Chocolate, Cocoa and Confectionery.
p. 151, Bernard W. Minifie.
The AVI Publishing Co., Westport, CT, 1980.

TO MAYNARD AND FLORENCE MACK
AND CAROLYN WILHELM BAKKE

ACKNOWLEDGMENT

There are many without whom this book would have been impossible. There are many others without whom it would have been a heck of a lot easier.

CONTENTS

*How to tell what's inside:
a simple rule of thumb.*

The Mayans and Aztecs made from the beans of the cacao tree a drink that they called *xocoatl*. The conquering Spanish returned home with *chocolate* (chō-cō-LAH-tay) in 1528. A royal wedding (in 1615) brought the drink to France, where they called it *chocolat* (shō-cō-LAH). It quickly crossed the Channel, and the English welcomed the *chocolata* (Stubbes, 1662), *jocolatte* (Pepys, 1664), *jacolatte* (Evelyn, 1682), and *chockelet* (Evelyn again, 1684).

In fact, it was not until chocolate came to the United States that people began spelling and pronouncing it correctly: CHOCOLATE.

THE CHOCOLATE ELITE

Research tells us that fourteen out of any ten individuals like chocolate. But what is "liking chocolate"? A flabby distinction at best. First of all, what is meant by "like"? There are many degrees of like.

DEGREES OF LIKE
(a graphic demonstration)

Q: Do you like chocolate?

Secondly, what is meant by "chocolate"? It could mean simply **chocolate**, or perhaps **chocolate**. Then there's **CHOCOLATE**, **CHOCOLATE**, **Chocolate**, *Chocolates*, and carob.

Or we may find among these chocolate-likers those who have no interest in candy per se, choosing instead to concentrate on chocolate cream pies, or brownies, or chocolate chip cookies, or chocolate soufflés, or chocolate fondue, or chocolate fudge, or chocolate sherbet, chocolate crêpes, chocolate cheesecake, chocolate nutballs, chocolate crunch, chocolate eclairs, chocolate waffles, chocolate mousse, chocolate croissants, chocolate ices, molé, chocolate bavarian, chocolate hot chocolate, chocolate yogurt, chocolate oatmeal, chocolate malts, chocolate salad, chocolate potato chips, chocolate pizza, chocolate cookies, chocolate turtles, chocolate chips, chocolate sundaes, chocolate bagels, chocolate trifle, chocolate omelets, Napoleons, dumplings, chocolate crackers, chocolate flan, chocolate Danish, hot fudge sundaes, chocolate graham crackers, chocolate fritters, chocolate he, chocolate pinwheels, chocolate eggplant, acks, chocolate cream puffs, chocolate tortes, oca, chocolate meringues, chocolate custard, ocolate frappes, chocolate parfaits, chocolate milk, chocolate pudding, chocolate spaghetti, milk shakes, chocolate sodas, chocolate pastry, muffins, chocolate doughnuts, chocolate pies, e cream, chocolate chili, chocolate bananas, e pretzels, Crème de Cacao, to name a few.

Certainly this book is not for everyone who merely claims to "like chocolate." It will serve little purpose for those who would just as soon have _____ as chocolate, or for those who cannot remember the last time they had chocolate, or who cannot anticipate within a reasonable time (three seconds) when the next occasion will be.
(ANY NOUN)

Rather, this book was written for the Chocolate Elite—

—the select millions who like chocolate in all its infinite variety, using "like" as in "I like to breathe."

The true connoisseur of chocolate shuns all chocolate novelty in favor of the uncompromised bittersweet experience. This is the *gourmet*.

At the other extreme is the individual who will embrace chocolate in any form: the *gourmand*.

And right in the middle of the field is she who is partial always to the gentleness and variety of milk chocolate: the *gourmoo*.

Part One
THE MANY FACES OF CHOCOLATE

CHOCOLATE PROFILE No. 1
The Pastoral Chocolatist

PROFILE: Pensive, pleasant, somewhat shy
FAVORITE TIME OF DAY: Midafternoon
FAVORITE SEASON: Summer
COLOR PREFERENCE: Yellow, green
SOCIAL ORIENTATION: Likes family gatherings
PREFERRED ACTIVITIES: Strolling, ruminating
CHOICE OF MUSIC: Lyrical
RELATIONSHIP WITH CHOCOLATE: Familiar
CHOICE OF CHOCOLATE: Milk

ABOUT MILK CHOCOLATE

Milk chocolate is made of at least ten percent chocolate liquor ("raw" chocolate pressed from cacao nibs) and twelve percent milk solids, combined with sugar, cocoa butter (the fat from the nibs), and vanilla. The finished chocolate usually comes in bars, although there are many novelty shapes such as

chocolate rabbits

Hershey's Kisses

Godiva's 14-inch model Learjet kit

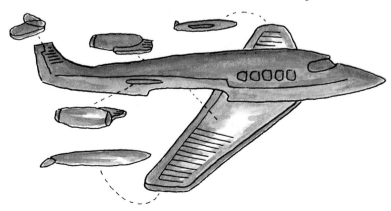

and glove compartment chocolate.

Many "fun forms" of milk chocolate will disappoint the discerning chocolatist since the manufacturer considers the shape, not the chocolate, to be the primary lure. (Although even the shapes are not always as appealing as the manufacturer imagines.)

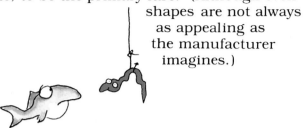

This marketing emphasis on Conceptual Appeal (gimmicks) means that the quality of the chocolate itself may be iffy. And even if the chocolate is good, there may yet be a cruel letdown awaiting the unwary consumer: Since most molded chocolate is hollow, the appearance of chocolate volume is often misleading.

Milk chocolate bars are a better bet for hard-core enjoyment.

Even the standard bars come in an impressive variety of sizes and shapes, from Hershey's Miniatures to the ever-popular Chunky to Ghirardelli's five-pound World's Biggest Chocolate Bar. (There is some evidence that this claim is not strictly accurate.)

Milk chocolate bar—large size

Beloved for its gentleness and simplicity, milk chocolate seems to proliferate like almost nothing else.

Beyond the astonishing range of all-milk-chocolate shapes and sizes, there is also an impressive variety of combination candy bars that feature milk chocolate: It encases savory peanut butter, fluffy nougat, sumptuous caramel-nut mixtures, delicate marshmallow, crispy rice, exquisite strawberry cream, sun-sweetened raisins, luscious pralines, you name it.

Cynics, of course, do not appreciate milk chocolate. Such is the price of widespread popularity.

THE BIRTH OF MILK CHOCOLATE

Although drinking chocolate was a well-established activity by the latter part of the nineteenth century, "eating chocolate" (introduced by Fry and Sons in 1847) was still somewhat of a novelty. Daniel Peter, famed Swiss chocolatier, was inspired to try to improve the smoothness and taste of the new candy.

Peter's idea was to combine some other ingredient with chocolate to balance its rough flavor. Naturally, his first thought was, "What does Switzerland have in abundance that I could use to process with chocolate?" His answer: Cheese. The resulting experiment was notoriously unsuccessful.

A number of ill-fated mixtures (grass, edelweiss, watch movements, numbered bank accounts) followed. In fact, no one actually knows how, in 1874, Peter finally stumbled on the answer, although there is some evidence that the simple suggestion of a neighbor ("Moo.") was the crucial catalyst.

Daniel Peter

Unidentified Collaborator

CHOCOLATE PROFILE No. 2
The Genteel Theobromian

PROFILE: Affable leader, secretly cynical
FAVORITE TIME OF DAY: Dusk
FAVORITE SEASON: Winter
COLOR PREFERENCE: Blue
SOCIAL ORIENTATION: Enjoys discussion groups and committees
PREFERRED ACTIVITIES: Philosophizing, analytical digression
CHOICE OF MUSIC: Baroque
RELATIONSHIP WITH CHOCOLATE: Bingeful
CHOICE OF CHOCOLATE: Sweet, semisweet

ABOUT SWEET AND SEMISWEET CHOCOLATE

Sweet and semisweet chocolate are made from fifteen to thirty-five percent chocolate liquor, plus sugar, cocoa butter, and vanilla. There is no precise distinction between these two types of chocolate; although it would seem that sweet chocolate should have less bitter liquor and more sugar than semisweet, often a chocolate labeled "sweet" (Maillard's Eagle Sweet, for example) tastes more bitter than one labeled "semisweet" (Zaanland Semisweet).

Unfortunately, the terminology is bound to remain somewhat of a mystery to consumers, since chocolate manufacturers are reluctant to reveal the complex methods by which they determine how they will label a given dark chocolate bar.

███ SWEET

███ SEMISWEET

Because of the imprecision of the two terms, sweet and semisweet chocolate are commonly lumped together as "dark" or "plain."

In general, dark chocolate is more straightforward, less playful than milk chocolate. Those who favor dark chocolate have little patience with cute candy.

This more serious approach is reflected not only in the dearth of fun shapes, but also in the size of plain chocolate bars: they rarely come small.

What greater pleasure than to savor a heavy volume
of the world's noblest achievements?

Dark chocolate also has a large following among dessert makers.

Although brownies and cakes most often call for unsweetened "baking chocolate," many other fine desserts—including fondues, croissants, mousses, and soufflés—specify dark chocolate. And semisweet chocolate shavings grace many a fancy torte.

Perhaps the most noteworthy of all dark chocolate's contributions to dessert making is the semisweet chocolate chip. Chocolate chips were originally manufactured by the Nestlé Company specifically for use in Ruth Wakefield's 1930 invention, Toll House Chocolate Crunch Cookies. These cookies are still the most common vehicle for the chips, but they continue to inspire many other creative uses as well.

POKER VARIATION

Use semisweet chocolate chips instead of plastic ones. This game requires considerably more control of facial muscles than ordinary poker: With one impetuous move, you could wipe out your entire earnings, even while holding a royal flush.

ON ICE CREAM

Any thorough chocolate researcher cannot fail to notice a bewildering characteristic common among those who love dark chocolate: They generally prefer vanilla ice cream to chocolate ice cream. This fact is not widely known because every vanilla-ice-cream-preferring-lover-of-dark-chocolate imagines that this unlikely preference must be a personal character flaw. Embarrassment, shame, and silence result.

Because vanilla ice cream accounts for fifty-five percent of all ice cream sales, compared to chocolate ice cream's measly nine percent, careless statisticians conclude that "vanilla is a more popular flavoring than chocolate." These researchers have not taken into account the unpublicized but documentable fact that a significant proportion of chocophiles do not take to chocolate ice cream. Given this, it would be more accurate to conclude that the shortcoming is not in chocolate, but in ice cream's faulty rendition of it.

chocolate!

Oh come off it.

CHOCOLATE PROFILE No. 3
The Refined Palette

PROFILE: Artistic, intellectual, reclusive
FAVORITE TIME OF DAY: Late evening
FAVORITE SEASON: Fall
COLOR PREFERENCE: Gray
SOCIAL ORIENTATION: Shuns company
PREFERRED ACTIVITIES: Painting, reading
CHOICE OF MUSIC: Symphonic
RELATIONSHIP WITH CHOCOLATE: Formal, but
    intense
CHOICE OF CHOCOLATE: Bittersweet

ABOUT BITTERSWEET AND BITTER CHOCOLATE

BITTERSWEET CHOCOLATE

Although many prefer more mellow, simple strains, a select audience appreciates the sharp, fine intensity of bittersweet bars.

For these discriminating few, chocolate is not so much a physical indulgence as a metaphysical experience. The disciple of bittersweet looks beyond the sensuous to chocolate's spiritual qualities, and finds there an aura, a mystique, a *mythos* second only to Motherhood.

"Arrangement in Black, Gray and Brown"

Those who have this commitment to "Chocolate for Chocolate's Sake" hesitate to allow other ingredients to compromise its purity: Bittersweet usually contains around fifty percent chocolate liquor.

Because of its distinct "bite," true bittersweet offers a marked advantage over other kinds of chocolate: Almost no one will ask more than once to share it with you.

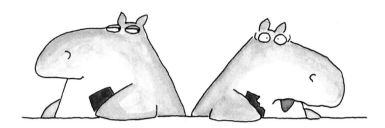

For those who strive to attain the highest level of chocolate consciousness—and to further minimize their exposure to "friends of convenience"—it is worthwhile to develop a taste for completely unsweetened chocolate.

BITTER CHOCOLATE

Bitter chocolate or "unsweetened" chocolate is simply hardened chocolate liquor or "mass." It is used for baking, and is therefore sometimes referred to as "baking chocolate" or "baker's chocolate."*

---

*"Baker's chocolate" should not be confused with "Baker's® Chocolate", which refers to any chocolate made by Walter Baker and Company.** Included among the company's chocolate products is, in fact, baker's chocolate, but there is a possibility of confusion since they also make sweetened chocolate, such as Baker's® German's® Sweet Chocolate.***
BRAND

baker's chocolate

Baker's® Chocolate

"Walter Baker and Company" is actually the name of a company founded not by Walter Baker but by his grandfather, Dr. James Baker, in 1779. It's now really just General Foods.**

This is actually not sweet chocolate. It's bittersweet. The "Sweet" does not modify "Chocolate" (German's *Sweet Chocolate*) but in fact is modified by "German's"** (*German's Sweet* Chocolate).

****General [do not read "Four-Star General"; those are asterisks] Foods means "foods in general", not foods *for* generals. (GF used to own Kohner Toys, which were not generally edible.)

*****"German" in this case has nothing to do with Germany. It is the surname of an American (Samuel German) whose idea it was (in 1852) to add sugar to baking chocolate before selling it, thus increasing convenience to bakers and profit to the manufacturer—in this case Baker's.*

| *a baker* | *general foods* | *a general* | *General Foods* | *a German* |

CHOCOLATE PROFILE No. 4
The Sensuous Chocophile

PROFILE: Moody, impulsive, self-indulgent
FAVORITE TIME OF DAY: Late morning (2 P.M. or so)
FAVORITE SEASON: Spring
COLOR PREFERENCE: Lavender by day, red by night
SOCIAL ORIENTATION: Likes visitors
PREFERRED ACTIVITIES: Lounging, bathing, dining
CHOICE OF MUSIC: Romantic
RELATIONSHIP WITH CHOCOLATE: Extremely cordial
CHOICE OF CHOCOLATE: Chocolates

CREAMS
AND VARIATIONS

Whoever said, "The best things in life are free," was, of course, just kidding. The best things go for $6.50 a pound and up.

"Chocolates" refers to any assortment of bite-size, chocolate-covered, overpriced candies. Most chocolates are given as gifts—for birthdays and anniversaries, as gestures of gratitude or appreciation or manipulation, and especially to further romance.

*A gift of chocolate can be an eloquent expression of
the true extent and nature of a lover's passion.*

Usually chocolates come preselected in decorative cardboard boxes or tins, but many shops that specialize in chocolates will allow you to assemble your assortment piece by piece.

In theory, the advantage of choosing your own is that you know what you are getting. Yet often chocolates lovers are as baffled by labeled chocolates as by mystery assortments. Too ashamed to admit ignorance, these unfortunate individuals are doomed to an endless procession of the familiar—caramels, nuts, and cream centers.

One chocolate with an elusive definition is the *cordial*. Many chocolates consumers are unclear as to whether the term "cordial" means that the filling is alcoholic. There are two basic answers to this:

And any chocolates enthusiast should know that *truffles* are the finest chocolates possible. Nevertheless, many devotees shun truffles out of sheer ignorance. A chocolate truffle is *not* made by coating fleshy, edible, potato-shaped fungi that grow underground. It is called "truffle" because it looks something like a regular old truffle, and because it, too, is a delicacy, and because it is hunted down in much the same way as its fungal counterpart.

Sniffing out truffles

This still does not explain what a chocolate truffle *is*. It has something to do with heavy cream and bittersweet chocolate and frenetic whipping. If you want a more precise definition, consult an expert.

HOW CHOCOLATES ARE MADE

There are four principal methods of coating various centers with chocolate.

The least expensive and most common method is *enrobing*: A conveyor belt carries the centers through a machine that showers them with chocolate.

The second process is *panning*: Chocolate is sprayed onto centers (commonly nuts and raisins) as they rotate in revolving pans, then cool air is blown into the pan to harden the coating.

There is also the "frontier method" of panning.

The third technique is *dipping*. Since dipping is most often done by hand, this process is generally used only by small-scale producers of fine chocolates. However, some larger manufacturers have devised ingenious ways of synthesizing the handmade look of dipped chocolates.

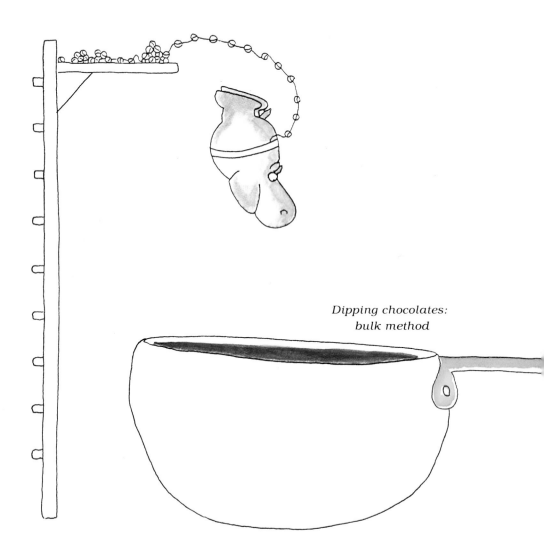

Dipping chocolates:
bulk method

The fourth and most sophisticated method of making chocolates is *shell-molding.* It is by this method that most "sculptural chocolates" are made, chocolates that masquerade as grape clusters or violins or sailboats or walnuts or what have you. (Never shells.)

This is how shell-molding is done:

SHELL PLANT PRODUCTION SEQUENCE

Filling	Shaking	Shell Forming		
		TURNOVER	OSCILLATION	VIBRATION
First Shell Cooler	Scraper	Second Shell Cooler	Center Filling	Liqueur Leveling
Center Cooler	Rim Warmer	Bottoming	Final Cooler	Demolding

By this method a manufacturer can make three to five pieces of candy a week. Shell-molded chocolates are priced accordingly.

HOW TO TELL
WHAT'S INSIDE

(Centers of Controversy)

There seems to be a certain moralistic streak in many chocolatiers, and consequently many boxed assortments are miniature "lessons in life," implying such wisdom as: *No pleasure is bought without some risk and disappointment.* This explains marshmallow nougat and pineapple jellies.

And yet these chocolate makers are not without their sense of fair play. As a sporting gesture, they mark each piece of candy with a squiggle or "signature" that identifies its contents. For example:

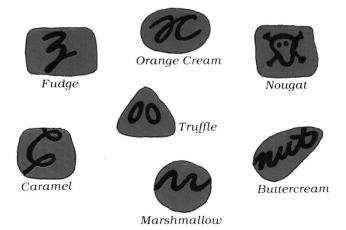

Fudge

Orange Cream

Nougat

Truffle

Caramel

Marshmallow

Buttercream

For those who do not feel up to the challenge of chocolate-reading, the more traditional method of center-determining is as follows: Stick your finger in the bottom. Put yucky ones back in the box.

CHOCOLATE PROFILE No. 5
The Vanilla Personality

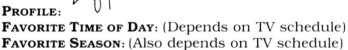

PROFILE:
FAVORITE TIME OF DAY: (Depends on TV schedule)
FAVORITE SEASON: (Also depends on TV schedule)
COLOR PREFERENCE: Fuchsia, chartreuse
SOCIAL ORIENTATION: Backward
PREFERRED ACTIVITIES: TV, carob-bean cruises
CHOICE OF MUSIC: AM radio
RELATIONSHIP WITH CHOCOLATE: Mutual antipathy
CHOICE OF CHOCOLATE: White

ABOUT WHITE CHOCOLATE AND CAROB

WHITE CHOCOLATE

There is some disagreement over whether white chocolate is "real" chocolate. Its ingredients—cocoa butter, sugar, milk solids, vanilla—are largely the same as those in milk chocolate, but without the chocolate liquor. Anyone who would claim that the absence of the liquor disqualifies white chocolate as chocolate is quibbling; the same purist would probably argue that fructose and water is not "real" orange juice.

White chocolate has great appeal for those who find that color and flavor interfere with the experience of texture.

Buying white chocolate is somewhat risky. Most chocolate has to conform to ingredient guidelines set by the Food and Drug Administration; white chocolate does not. And since it is most often sold not in prepackaged bars but in chunks (called "break-up"), there is frequently no ingredient label on it. You could, therefore, unwittingly purchase as "white chocolate" a candy made of sugar, milk, vanilla, and congealed vegetable fat.

However, the very best white chocolate is easy to identify. It has an ivory color like this:

It smells like this:

(scratch and sniff)

And it tastes like this:

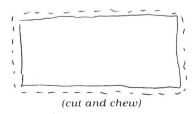

(cut and chew)

CAROB

Carob is a brown powder made from the pulverized fruit of a Mediterranean evergreen. Some consider carob an adequate substitute for chocolate because it has some similar nutrients (calcium, phosphorus), and because it can, when combined with vegetable fat and sugar, be made to approximate the color and consistency of chocolate. Of course, the same arguments can as persuasively be made in favor of dirt.

There are quite a number of other "imitation chocolate" products. For a fuller discussion of these, see elsewhere.

**SEX AND CHOCOLATE:
WHICH IS BETTER?**

Part Two
THE PHYSIOLOGY AND PSYCHOLOGY OF CHOCOPHILIA

CHOCOLATE, TOBLERONE SWISS MILK CHOCOLATE WITH ALMOND A
HARD SWISS SEMI-SWEET CHOCOLATE WITH SPLIT ALMONDS, LINDT BITT
AFTER EIGHT DARK CHOCOLATE COVERED THIN MINTS, COTE D'OR CHOO
AIT, ELITE BITTER-SWEET CHOCOLATE, WHITMAN'S SWEET DARK CHOCOLA
WEET CHOCOLATE, BAKER'S GERMAN'S SWEET CHOCOLATE, MAILLARD EAGI
HERSHEY'S SPECIAL DARK, WHITMAN'S SAMPLER, PERUGINA GIANDUIA CH(
ERSWEET CHOCOLATE APPLE, SAROTTI BITTERE SAHNE-SCHOKOLADE, GHIR
ATE MUNCHY MALT, TOBLER EXTRA BITTERSWEET SWISS CHOCOLATE, I
CHOCOLATE, LANVIN PASTRY-COOKING CHOCOLATE, KRON GOLFBALLS, C(
AIN CHOCOLATE, M&M'S PLAIN CHOCOLATE CANDIES, CADBURY'S MILK CH(
CHOCOLATE, LINDT SWISS MILK CHOCOLATE, CHUNKY MILK CHOCOLATE, H(
Y'S FIVE CENTRES, WHITMAN'S MILK CHOCOLATE WITH ALMONDS, Z

FACT: Chocolate reaches a higher level
of consciousness, *in minutes*, than the other
leading analgesic.

HERE'S SCIENTIFIC PROOF:

ASPIRIN

CHOCOLATE

X

X

CHOCOLATE CANDIES, CADBURY'S MILK CHOCOLATE, WILBUR MILK CHO
MILK MILK CHOCOLATE, CHUNKY MILK CHOCOLATE, HERSHEY'S KRACKE
, WHITMAN'S MILK CHOCOLATE WITH ALMONDS, BAKER'S UNSWEETENEI
EL EDEL-BITTER, DROSTE COFFEE MILK CHOCOLATE, ZAANLAND MILK CHO
SH TOFFEE, PERUGINA'S MILK CHOCOLATE, HERSHEY'S MR. GOODBAR, I
GEL BITTER SWEET CHOCOLATE, COTE D'OR HIGH QUALITY PLAIN CHO
SSES, SAROTTI PLAIN CHOCOLATE, LINDT CHOCOLETTI, TOBLER TRADITION
IQUEUR CUPS, TEUSCHER ASSORTED TRUFFLES, LI-LAC ALMOND BARK, B
M&M'S PEANUT CHOCOLATE CANDIES, HERSHEY'S MILK CHOCOLATE, TOI
HOCOLATE WITH ALMOND AND HONEY NOUGAT, SUCHARD SWISS SEMI-SWE
PLIT ALMONDS, LINDT BITTERSWEET CHOCOLATE, AFTER EIGHT DARK CH
N MINTS, COTE D'OR CHOCOLAT SUPERIEUR AU LAIT, ELITE BITTER-SWI

YOUR BODY AND CHOCOLATE

Anything that is greatly admired is bound to be much maligned as well. Chocolate is no exception. There always seems to be someone looking over your shoulder, just waiting for an opportunity to lecture on The Darker Side of Chocolate.

The following point-by-point refutation of the many pervasive and insidious myths should help silence the critics and put you at peace with your chocolate.

MYTH No. 1
"Chocolate is bad for your teeth."

This criticism can be effectively defused by simply quoting from the recent report of a Massachusetts Institute of Technology research team:

"In contrast to popular expectations, cocoa powder has exhibited a significant caries-inhibitory effect when added to cariogenic diets in animal studies... The conclusion drawn... is that there is a heat-stable, water-soluble chemical component of cocoa which shows an inhibitory effect upon total dextran synthesis of _streptococcus mutans_."*

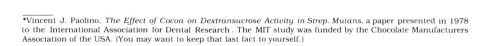

*Vincent J. Paolino, *The Effect of Cocoa on Dextransucrose Activity in Strep. Mutans*, a paper presented in 1978 to the International Association for Dental Research. The MIT study was funded by the Chocolate Manufacturers Association of the USA. (You may want to keep that last fact to yourself.)

MYTH No. 2
"Chocolate is fattening."

A crucial factor has been overlooked in this widespread condemnation of chocolate: Most chocolate eaters tend to supplement their chocolate intake with other foods. By what right, what logic can chocolate be singled out as the cause of plumpness? How can we be certain that, say, carrots are not a catalyst to weight-gain when chocolate is present?

And there is empirical evidence that also raises serious doubts about chocolate's fatteningness: Few chocolate lovers can simply lie back and wait for chocolate to come to them. For most, getting and keeping chocolate often requires strenuous physical work.

Selected Average Caloric Expenditures
Related to the Routine Pursuit and Maintenance
of Personal Chocolate Resources

ACTIVITY	CALORIC EXPENDITURE
Carrying seven pounds of chocolate from store to residence	359
Hiding all chocolate before answering door when company drops by unexpectedly	744
Swimming to Switzerland	497,562 (approx.)

MYTH No. 3
"Chocolate is a dangerous drug."

There is a long-standing controversy about the supposed ill-effects of chocolate on psychophysiological equilibrium. Critics of chocolate cite the pronounced mood swings of chocolate eaters, fluctuations that are theoretically caused by the caffeine, sugar, and theobromine in chocolate: These stimulants create an artificial high, soon followed by a precipitous descent to an artificial low.

THE STAGES OF CHOCOLATE ASSIMILATION
(a dramatization)

| START:
SUBJECT
IN NEUTRAL | STAGE 1:
FIRST
TASTE | STAGE 2:
HITTING THE
BLOODSTREAM | STAGE 3:
CHOCUPHORIA |

| STAGE 4:
GOING | STAGE 5:
GOING | STAGE 6:
GONE | STAGE 7:
ACUTE CHOCOLACK |

If, for argument's sake, we concede that chocolate ingestion may carry the risk of post-taste letdown, the solution is nevertheless obvious: To circumvent stage 7, begin the cycle again between stages 5 and 6.

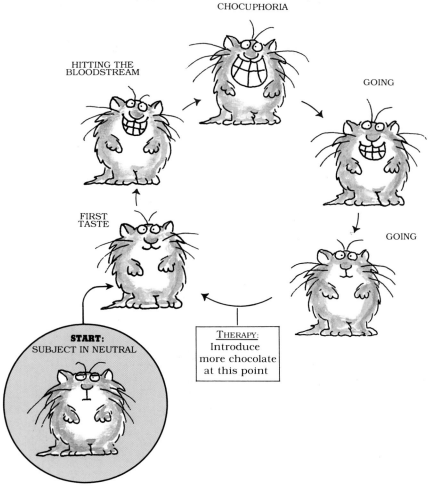

CHOCUPHORIA

HITTING THE
BLOODSTREAM

GOING

GOING

FIRST
TASTE

START:
SUBJECT IN NEUTRAL

THERAPY:
Introduce
more chocolate
at this point

This is, of course, a somewhat simplistic approach. A more comprehensive plan of action for physiopsychological well-being is delineated on the following pages.

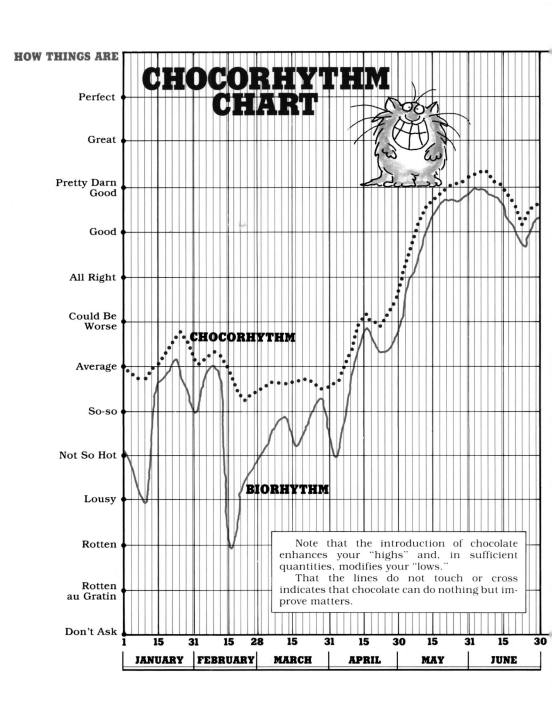

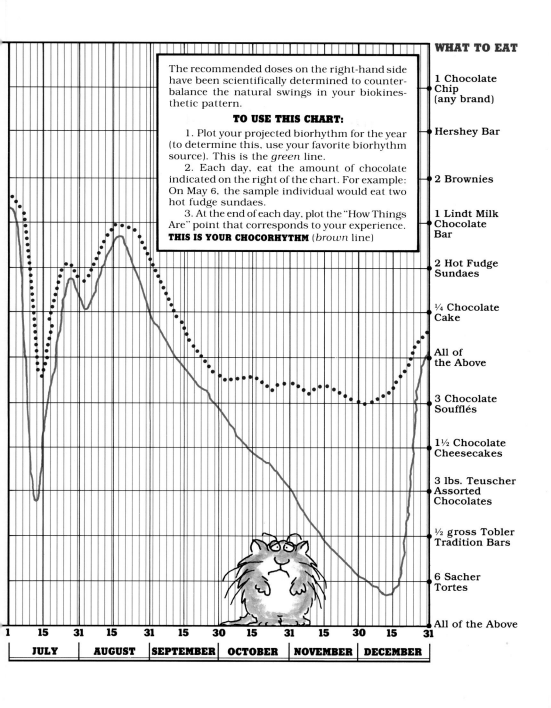

WHAT TO EAT

1 Chocolate Chip (any brand)

Hershey Bar

2 Brownies

1 Lindt Milk Chocolate Bar

2 Hot Fudge Sundaes

¼ Chocolate Cake

All of the Above

3 Chocolate Soufflés

1½ Chocolate Cheesecakes

3 lbs. Teuscher Assorted Chocolates

½ gross Tobler Tradition Bars

6 Sacher Tortes

All of the Above

The recommended doses on the right-hand side have been scientifically determined to counterbalance the natural swings in your biokinesthetic pattern.

TO USE THIS CHART:

1. Plot your projected biorhythm for the year (to determine this, use your favorite biorhythm source). This is the *green* line.

2. Each day, eat the amount of chocolate indicated on the right of the chart. For example: On May 6, the sample individual would eat two hot fudge sundaes.

3. At the end of each day, plot the "How Things Are" point that corresponds to your experience. **THIS IS YOUR CHOCORHYTHM** (*brown* line)

1	15	31	15	31	15	30	15	31	15	30	15	31
JULY		AUGUST		SEPTEMBER		OCTOBER		NOVEMBER		DECEMBER		

MYTH No. 4
"Chocolate
is not nutritious."

Chocolate is categorically excluded from any listing of beneficial foods, on the grounds that "it is not good for you." But a quick glance at this nutritional comparison of chocolate with other so-called "healthy" snacks suggests otherwise.

NUTRITIVE COMPARISON CHART

	Carrots	Yogurt	Apples	Peanut Butter	Grapes	Cottage Cheese	Milk Chocolate with Almonds
Serving Size	several shreds	1 tbl.	½ slice	1 tsp.	1	6 curds	8 1-oz. bars
B-1 Thiamine MG.	(trace)	(trace)	(trace)	.01	(trace)	(trace)	.16
B-2 Riboflavin MG.	(trace)	0.1	(trace)	0.1	(trace)	0.1	.96
Niacin MG.	.03	.04	.01	.8	.01	(trace)	1.6
Vitamin A I.U.	550.0	16.5	4.24	12.5	37.5	.8	560.0
Iron MG.	.04	.01	.02	.01	.02	.01	4.0
Phosphorus MG.	(trace)	26.2	.01	14.0	1.5	.01	616.0
Potassium MG.	1.0	39.0	4.0	22.0	6.0	8.0	768.0
Calcium MG.	1.9	31.12	.25	3.7	.81	4.2	520.0
Protein G.	(trace)	.5	(trace)	1.5	.06	.63	20.8

MYTH No. 5

"Chocolate is nothing more than a substitute for affection."

Much has been made lately of the recent scientific finding that there is a chemical in chocolate—phenylethylamine—that is virtually identical to the substance manufactured by the brain of an infatuated individual. In various studies of this phenomenon,* the conclusion drawn is that chocolate obsession is in fact self-medication for the spurned lover. He or she is trying to synthesize the "high" of being in love.

As is too often the case with these social scientists, they are taking sound, highly suggestive data and drawing empirically absurd conclusions. What reasonable soul prefers romance to truffles?

Clearly it is not the lovelorn sufferer who seeks solace in chocolate, but rather the chocolate-deprived individual who, desperate, seeks in mere love a pale approximation of bittersweet euphoria.

---

*Drs. Donald F. Klein and Michael R. Liebowitz, "Hysteroid Dysphoria," *Psychiatric Clinics of North America*, Vol. II, No. 3, Dec. 1979; Dr. John Money, *Love and Love-Sickness: The Science of Sex, Gender Difference and Pair-Bonding*, Johns Hopkins University Press, 1980.

MYTH No. 6
"Chocolate is bad for your complexion."

This claim is completely without scientific substantiation. In fact, there are many quite weighty individuals who believe that just the opposite is true.

MYTH NO. 7
"Chocolate is an aphrodisiac."

Actually this is true.

SOME PROVOCATIVE OBSERVATIONS

The greatest tragedies were written by the Greeks and by Shakespeare. Neither knew chocolate.

The Swiss are known for nonviolence. They are also known for superb chocolate.

AVOIDING NON-CHOCOLATE SITUATIONS

Politely decline all wedding invitations.
Weddings are notorious for white cake
with white icing.

CHOCOLATE AND THE MIND

PSYCHE AND CHOCOLATE

Chocolate can do wonderful things for your overall sense of well-being. It can offset disappointments, allay frustrations, provide joy and comfort —even inspire romance.

> I want to nibble on your ear...

But any serious relationship with chocolate is not without its trials. Fear of separation gnaws at anyone deeply involved with chocolate; financial difficulties are unquestionably exacerbated by the love of chocolate; and there ever lurks the dread that your hard-won happiness will be compromised by the unwanted attentions of others.

If you are truly committed to making your relationship with chocolate a dynamic and satisfying one, you have to be prepared to work at it. Some guidelines follow for achieving meaningfulness.

1. FIND TIME ALONE TOGETHER

Chocolate was never meant to be shared.

2. AVOID SUDDEN OR PROLONGED SEPARATIONS

An abrupt, unexpected, or extended separation can cause considerable hardship. Make every effort to have your chocolate with you, even if it seems impractical.

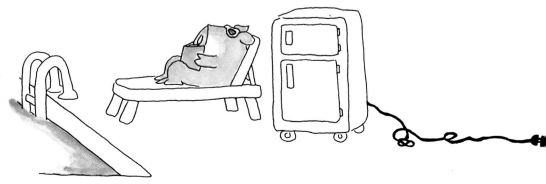

3. TAKE TIME TO LISTEN

Often chocolate has something to say that only you can hear.

4. MINIMIZE FINANCIAL PRESSURES

If you are experiencing any financial difficulties, chocolate loving will most likely make them worse. The economic outlook for chocophiles is bleak.

1948—5¢ bar

1979—25¢ bar

2000 (projected)—$64.85 bar

And mortgage money for chocolate remains tight.

But the resourceful chocolatist will not let money troubles stand in the way of fulfillment. If chocolate cannot be bought, it may still be won by charm

or ingenuity.

If you take care to keep in mind the foregoing guidelines, your chocolate-based conflicts will be greatly reduced. Nevertheless, it is important to realize above all that no relationship ever goes entirely smoothly. There will always be times when you and your chocolate simply aren't hitting it off.

When this happens, you must not overreact. Keep calm, maintain your perspective. This time will pass. Perhaps the best thing you can do is to go off by yourself for a while and try to imagine what your life would be like without chocolate.

BEING PREPARED FOR THE WORST

If the remotest possibility exists that you could become
snowbound, take this simple precaution:

Remove and discard all insulation from ski jacket.
Replace with 7 lbs. (approx.) shaved chocolate.
Resew seams.

**WARNING: NEVER WARM UP IN FRONT OF A FIRE
WITHOUT FIRST REMOVING JACKET.**

INTELLECT AND CHOCOLATE

Much serious thought has been devoted to the subject of chocolate: What does chocolate *mean*? Is the pursuit of chocolate a right or a privilege? Does the notion of chocolate preclude the concept of free will?

Yet even these most provocative lines of inquiry seemed to blur when the Rational Skepticists first posed that profound and unsettling question,

How do we know that chocolate exists?

        This had everyone stumped (and not a little depressed) for quite some time.

Then the Empiricists came along and pointed out that of course what we *mean* by "knowing" is "that which we learn through our senses." For example, we *know* that chocolate exists because we can *taste* it.*

Some irksome individual—a Negativist—noted the resulting paradox: By the time the existence of chocolate is thus (that is, by tasting) confirmed, the chocolate no longer exists.

It was the Capitalists who first realized that it does not really matter whether chocolate truly exists or not, as long as people buy it.

*This still leaves open the deeper question of whether or not there exists a Supreme Bean.

IS THE CHOCOLATE AT ITS BEST?

As with most fine things, chocolate has its season. There is a simple memory aid that you can use to determine whether it is the correct time to order chocolate dishes:

ANY MONTH WHOSE NAME CONTAINS THE LETTER A, E, OR U IS THE PROPER TIME FOR CHOCOLATE.

Part Three
KNOWING YOUR CHOCOLATE

In taste tests conducted nationwide, chocolate lovers were blindfolded and asked to compare five leading brands of chocolate. The result?

3 OUT OF 4 INDIVIDUALS ACTUALLY RESENTED HAVING BEEN BLINDFOLDED

EVALUATING CHOCOLATE

There is a certain amount of expertise that serious chocolatists ought to acquire in order to enhance their *ecstasis chocolati*. Experts judge the quality of chocolate by the following criteria:

PRESENTATION This means how it looks. The chocolate should have an even, glossy surface. Lack of shine indicates staleness and/or questionable moral character.

SNAP This term refers to the way the chocolate performs under pressure. Good chocolate should have a spunky, decisive break. If it splinters, it is too dry; if it breaks reluctantly, it is too waxy; if it folds, something is definitely wrong.

MOUTH FEEL This somewhat unpoetic phrase is used by experts to mean texture. The "mouth feel" of chocolate (dry/gritty; moist/smooth) depends mostly on how long the chocolate has been *conched*, i.e. made smooth by slopping around in shell-shaped vats. Chocolate that wears away more than twenty percent of your tongue has not been conched long enough. Chocolate that slides down your throat before you have had a chance to taste it has been overconched or "conched out."

Note: Judging the texture of chocolate by "hand feel" is not recommended.

TASTE This is the word used by the Very Knowledgeable Indeed to mean "taste." There are three primary components of taste by which an authority will judge chocolate:

1. **Sweetness**—mostly due to percentage of sugar.
2. **Chocolatitude** (chocolateyness)—mostly due to percentage of chocolate liquor.
3. **Bouquet**—due to quality of beans, roasting time, and blending formula.

Often the taste of chocolate is most affected by a fourth factor: **Price** (mostly due to gall of manufacturer). A "high price" enhances the flavor of received chocolate, but undermines the flavor of bought chocolate.

Using the above criteria—presentation, snap, mouth feel, and taste—a panel of experts will generally agree on the character of a given brand of chocolate.

Q: HOW WOULD YOU DESCRIBE CADBURY'S MILK CHOCOLATE ?

However, there will rarely be any consensus on the quality of that same chocolate.

Q: ON A SCALE OF 1 TO 10, HOW WOULD YOU RANK CADBURY'S MILK CHOCOLATE?

Clearly you will have to learn to judge for yourself.

HOW TO STORE YOUR CHOCOLATE

Chocolate lasts longest if kept in a cool, airtight container.

HANDLING CHOCOLATE

THE PROPERTIES OF CHOCOLATE

Chocolate is quite temperamental, and requires cautious handling. You can minimize the frustrations of chocolate care by becoming familiar with its standard patterns of behavior:

If stored at cold temperatures (below 55°F), chocolate *sweats* when brought too quickly to room temperature.

At warm temperatures (above 85°F), chocolate may *bloom*: The cocoa butter rises to the surface and produces a whitish film.

At warmer temperatures (90°–220°F), chocolate *melts*.

At high temperatures (above 220°F), chocolate *burns*.

In the heat of commerce (Dow Jones Industrial Average 4,000 or above), chocolate *conglomerates.*

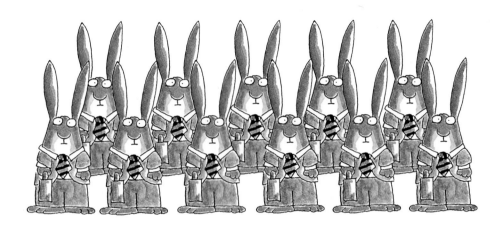

It is usually very difficult to determine if chocolate has conglomerated. The taste of the chocolate may be affected, but its appearance will remain deceptively the same. You might find this chart informative:

PARENT COMPANY	OWNS
NABISCO	Mercken's
GOLDEN GRAIN (**Rice-A-Roni**)	Ghirardelli
CAMPBELL SOUP CO.	Godiva USA, Pepperidge Farm
PET FOODS, INC.	Whitman's, Stuckey's
MULTIFOOD	Tobler, Suchard
CADBURY-SCHWEPPES LTD.	Cadbury's
THE NESTLÉ COMPANY	(most of the known world)

KEEPING YOUR CHOCOLATE FRESH

Chocolate is not only sensitive to temperature, but to its social environment as well. If chocolate associates too freely with other influential foods, its taste will inevitably be compromised.

Because of the impressionable nature of chocolate, it is advisable not to store it in your refrigerator. For short-term storage, a cool, dry cabinet is best; for longer keeping, wrap the chocolate well and hide it in your freezer.

The most conscientious individuals will see to it that storage is not a problem.

HOW TO MAKE CHOCOLATE STAINS DISAPPEAR

REMOVAL OF CHOCOLATE FROM POROUS MATERIAL

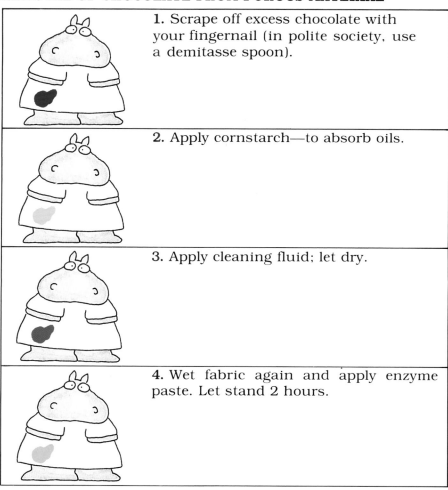

1. Scrape off excess chocolate with your fingernail (in polite society, use a demitasse spoon).

2. Apply cornstarch—to absorb oils.

3. Apply cleaning fluid; let dry.

4. Wet fabric again and apply enzyme paste. Let stand 2 hours.

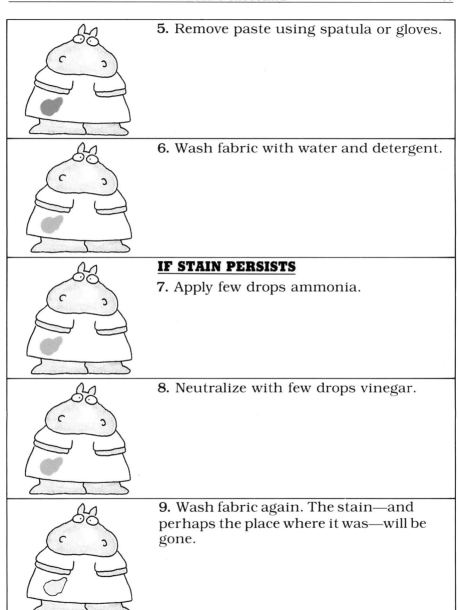

5. Remove paste using spatula or gloves.

6. Wash fabric with water and detergent.

IF STAIN PERSISTS

7. Apply few drops ammonia.

8. Neutralize with few drops vinegar.

9. Wash fabric again. The stain—and perhaps the place where it was—will be gone.

ALTERNATE METHOD OF STAIN OBLITERATION

1. Melt ¼ pound chocolate for each pound of fabric.

2. Immerse fabric in chocolate and let stand.

3. Rinse well.

REMOVAL OF CHOCOLATE FROM NONPOROUS MATERIAL

These spots are easily licked.

A SPECIAL NOTE FOR BUSHWHACKERS

If you love wilderness exploration; your nature is not easily compatible with something as delicate as chocolate. Yet there is a chocolate bar made especially with the outdoor adventurer in mind: Hershey's Tropical Bar. Whereas conventional chocolate bars are too frail to withstand heat, moisture, and proximity to baked beans, the Tropical Bar has been formulated for endurance: It has substantially less cocoa butter than ordinary chocolate bars. This gives it the keeping qualities of wax. Also the taste.

Yet although the Tropical Bar may not have the flavor appeal of other chocolate, there is no denying its practical value to campers.

CROSSING THE DESSERT

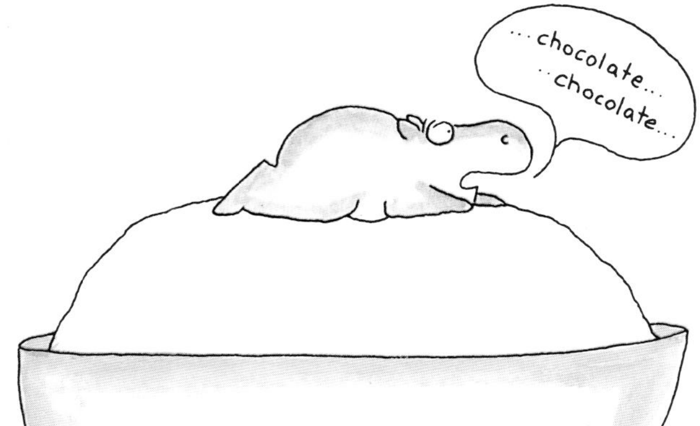

MAKING THINGS WITH CHOCOLATE

Chocolate cookery would seem to be the perfect pastime for those devoted to chocolate. Unfortunately, this is not the case. Although the element of prolonged close interaction with chocolate is certainly agreeable to the chocolate sensibility, the element of time is highly incompatible with it. Chocolate enthusiasts are not known for their patience.

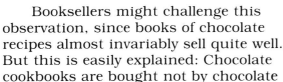

Booksellers might challenge this observation, since books of chocolate recipes almost invariably sell quite well. But this is easily explained: Chocolate cookbooks are bought not by chocolate

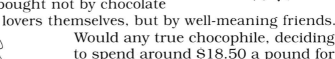

lovers themselves, but by well-meaning friends. Would any true chocophile, deciding to spend around $18.50 a pound for something rectangular, heavy, and strongly reminiscent of chocolate, buy a book?

The recipes that follow take a low frustration threshold into account. All but one* are short but sweet.

---

*The exception, Advanced Chocolate Molding, is included both because of the significant volume of chocolate involved, and because it contains a feature unique among chocolate recipes: The calories expended in preparing it exceed the calories ingested in eating it.

NOTES ON MELTING CHOCOLATE

In any recipe calling for liquefied chocolate, care must be taken to melt the chocolate gradually.

Milk chocolate requires
even lower temperatures.

Do not allow any moisture to combine with the chocolate while you are melting it. A single drop may cause the mixture to suddenly stiffen.

BROWNIES

Yield: Immediately (Makes 24)

Preheat oven to 350° F.
In the top of a double boiler, melt together, then let cool:
 5 ounces bitter chocolate
 ½ cup butter
In a large bowl, beat well:
 3 eggs
Add gradually to eggs, and beat until foamy:
 ¾ cup white sugar
 1 cup light brown sugar
 2 teaspoons vanilla
Gently fold the cooled chocolate mixture into the egg mixture,
then add:
 1¼ cups all-purpose flour
Add:
 1 tablespoon vegetable oil
Stir in:
 1 cup pecan halves
Bake in a greased 9 × 13-inch pan for approximately 25 minutes.

TESTING FOR DONENESS: The brownies are done when an inserted
fork comes out clean.

HIPPO PÔT DE MOUSSE

In the top of a double boiler, melt:

4 ounces semisweet chocolate

2 ounces bittersweet chocolate

Let the chocolate cool for 5 minutes.

Meanwhile, whip together until very stiff:

1 pint heavy cream, well chilled

1 teaspoon almond extract

Gently fold the cooled chocolate into the whipped cream; there will be many flecks of chocolate in the mixture.

Spoon the dessert into 6 large wine glasses. Chill 1 hour.

Serves 1

CHOCOLATE CHIP COOKIE

Theoretical yield: 48 cookies, 2 inches each

Preheat oven to 375° F.
Cream together until light and fluffy:
    ¾ cup butter
    ¾ cup light brown sugar
    ¼ cup dark brown sugar
Beat in:
    1 egg
    1 teaspoon vanilla
Sift together, then stir into the butter mixture:
    1⅓ cups all-purpose flour
    ¾ teaspoon baking soda
Chop into pieces, then stir in:
    6 ounces bittersweet chocolate

It is traditional at this point to sample the batter before proceeding.

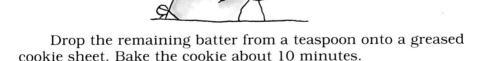

Drop the remaining batter from a teaspoon onto a greased cookie sheet. Bake the cookie about 10 minutes.

USING LEFTOVER CHOCOLATE

This is truly a delicious alternative
to your humdrum, everyday preparation of bugs.

NEVER-FAIL SOUFFLÉ

Make sure your oven temperature
is accurate, and keep the finished soufflé
away from drafts.

Chocolate Soufflé   *Chocolate Souffloppe*

MOLDING CHOCOLATE BUNNIES

Have ready (clean and dry) 10 plastic, metal, or unglazed ceramic bunny-shaped molds.
Over hot water or low flame, melt to 90°F:

5 pounds professional-quality coating chocolate

Pour the chocolate into the molds. Tap them gently on a hard surface to release air bubbles.
Place molds in a frost-free freezer until firm. Unmold.

OLD-FASHIONED METHOD

Stand on end:

1 block of chocolate, 4 × 4 × 7 feet

Chip away all pieces that do not contribute to an overall impression of rabbitittity.

ADVANCED CHOCOLATE MOLDING

To add just the right decorating touch to your holiday table, you can make this elegant and unusual centerpiece.

Find:

    1 medium-size lethargic pig

Place in its mouth:

    1 Droste bittersweet apple (sections glued together)

Grease the pig generously with:

    3 pounds softened unsalted butter

Note: If the pig becomes uncooperative at this point, you will have to abandon the project.

Leaving a seam around the vertical circumference, cover the pig with:

    Plaster of Paris

Let dry. Unmold. Thank the pig.

Fill the mold with:

    27 pounds melted coating chocolate

Let harden and unmold.

    Place the finished sculpture on a large serving platter; garnish with sprigs of holly and evergreens.

    Your friends and family may be talking about this for years to come!

SALVAGING
FAILED DESSERTS

It can be devastating to meet with failure after the exertion of cooking. This is all the more true when chocolate is a key ingredient in your recipe, since of course you cannot just throw the whole thing away.

If your chocolate dessert does not turn out, there are two things you can do to cut your losses:

1. You can hope no one notices.

2. You can use your imagination to find a way to turn the dessert into something else. For example:

☞ Unsuccessful fudge makes an excellent ice cream topping.
☞ Unsuccessful brownies make an unusual and delicious pudding.
☞ An unsuccessful chocolate soufflé makes an attractive beret.

Making your own
chocolate at home is a little extra
work, but well worth it.

Part Four
WHERE TO GET IT

MAKING YOUR OWN CHOCOLATE

In these times of economic hardship and worker alienation, perhaps you might consider growing, harvesting, and producing your own chocolate instead of relying on some huge, impersonal manufacturer. Here is how:

TO GROW THE BEANS

You will need:
> *1 small plantation*
> *4,000 or so cacao seedlings*
> *Time*

Instructions:
> **1.** Move to within 20° N or S of the Equator (on dry land).
> **2.** For each 5 lbs. of chocolate desired per year, plant 1 cacao seedling, locating each in the shade of a larger tree (banana, mango, etc.). Plant at a density of approx. 1,000 trees per hectare.
> **3.** Wait 5-8 years for the trees to mature.

Now you are ready to harvest.

TO HARVEST THE BEANS

You will need:

50 long-handled pod-whoppers
25 machetes
390 fermenting trays with burlap
Help

Instructions:

1. Using your long-handled pod-whoppers, gather all ripe pods. **Do Not Climb The Trees.**

2. Gently split the pods open with the machetes. Scoop out the beans.

3. Put the beans in trays in a draft-free area and cover with burlap. Let stand until the beans have turned medium brown (approx. 1 week).

4. Dry the beans in the sun, stirring occasionally until their moisture content is below 7% (approx. 3 days).

You are now ready to make chocolate. (Or to sell out the whole operation to some huge, impersonal manufacturer.)

TO MAKE CHOCOLATE LIQUOR

You will need:

1 cleaning machine
1 scale
1 roaster
1 cracker and fanner
1 grinding mill
Endurance

Instructions:

1. Pass the beans through your cleaning machine to remove dried pulp and other extraneous matter.

2. Weigh, select, and blend the beans as desired.

3. Roast the beans at 250°F for 2 hours.

4. Use your cracker and fanner to remove the shells from the beans, leaving the nibs.

5. Crush the nibs in your mill. The heat generated will liquefy the pulp, creating your chocolate "mass."

You now have the base raw material of all chocolate.

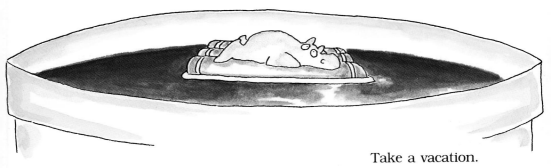

Take a vacation.

HARD SWISS SEMI-SWEET CHOCOLATE WITH SPLIT ALMONDS, LINDT BITT
AFTER EIGHT DARK CHOCOLATE COVERED THIN MINTS, COTE D'OR CHOC
AIT, ELITE BITTER-SWEET CHOCOLATE, WHITMAN'S SWEET DARK CHOCOLA
EET CHOCOLATE, BAKER'S GERMAN'S SWEET CHOCOLATE, MAILLARD EAGL
HERSHEY'S SPECIAL DARK, WHITMAN'S SAMPLER, PERUGINA GIANDUIA CHO
RSWEET CHOCOLATE APPLE, SAROTTI BITTERE SAHNE-SCHOKOLADE, GHIR
ATE MUNCHY MALT, TOBLER EXTRA BITTERSWEET SWISS CHOCOLATE,
CHOCOLATE, LANVIN PASTRY-COOKING CHOCOLATE, KRON GOLFBALLS, C
AIN CHOCOLATE, M&M'S PLAIN CHOCOLATE CANDIES, CADBURY'S MILK CHO
CHOCOLATE, LINDT SWISS MILK CHOCOLATE, CHUNKY MILK CHOCOLATE, H
Y'S FIVE CENTRES, WHITMAN'S MILK CHOCOLATE WITH ALMONDS, BA
HOCOLATE,   OLATE, Z
ATE, HEATH   HERSHEY'S
O MILKA, S   H QUALIT
HERSHEY'S   TTI, TO
VA CHOCOLA   , LI-LAC
GER NONPA   EY'S MIL
RONE SWISS   T, SUCHA
CHOCOLATE   ATE, AFT
ATE COVER   U LAIT, B
HOCOLATE,   MI SWEE
S GERMAN'   LATE, H
K, WHITMAN   TE BITT
PPLE, SAR   MILK CH
T, TOBLER   EL-BITT
N PASTRY-C   EXTRA D
M&M'S PLAI   ATE, WILB
LINDT SWIS   HEY'S I
ENTRES, W   Y'S UNSW
SPRENGEL E   NLAND M
H ENGLISH   MR. GOO
, SPRENGEL   ITY PLAI
Y'S KISSES, S   TRADITIO
IQUEUR CU   BARK, B
M&M'S PEA   ATE, TO
HOCOLATE   EMI-SWE
PLIT ALMON   DARK CH
N MINTS, C   TER-SWE
MAN'S SWEE   ATE, BAK
CHOCOLAT   S SPECIA
MPLER, PE   T CHOCO
BITTERE S   E MUNCH
A BITTER-S   OCOLATE
KING CHOCO   LAIN CHO

For many, it's a question of survival.

CHOCOLATE CANDIES, CADBURY'S MILK CHOCOLATE, WILBUR MILK CHO
MILK MILK CHOCOLATE, CHUNKY MILK CHOCOLATE, HERSHEY'S KRACK
, WHITMAN'S MILK CHOCOLATE WITH ALMONDS, BAKER'S UNSWEETENE
EL EDEL-BITTER, DROSTE COFFEE MILK CHOCOLATE, ZAANLAND MILK CHO
SH TOFFEE, PERUGINA'S MILK CHOCOLATE, HERSHEY'S MR. GOODBAR,
GEL BITTER SWEET CHOCOLATE, COTE D'OR HIGH QUALITY PLAIN CHO
SSES, SAROTTI PLAIN CHOCOLATE, LINDT CHOCOLETTI, TOBLER TRADITIO
IQUEUR CUPS, TEUSCHER ASSORTED TRUFFLES, LI-LAC ALMOND BARK, B
M&M'S PEANUT CHOCOLATE CANDIES, HERSHEY'S MILK CHOCOLATE, CH
HOCOLATE WITH ALMOND AND HONEY NOUGAT, SUCHARD SWISS SEMI-SWE
PLIT ALMONDS, LINDT BITTERSWEET CHOCOLATE, AFTER EIGHT DARK CH
N MINTS, COTE D'OR CHOCOLAT SUPERIEUR AU LAIT, ELITE BITTER-SWI
MAN'S SWEET DARK CHOCOLATE, ZAANLAND SEMI SWEET CHOCOLATE, BAK

SHOPPING FOR CHOCOLATE

GROCERY STORES

Freshness, variety, and low, low prices: three good reasons to avoid buying chocolate at grocery stores. These stores rob chocolate-buying of all its romance. The low prices deprive you of that vital sense of suffering and sacrifice for your chocolate; the sheer abundance makes your purchase appear trivial; the relentless freshness tells you that many others have been here before you, and this makes your own intimate relationship with chocolate seem tawdry and cheap.

DEPARTMENT STORES

Many of the tonier department stores are now devoting entire
sections to chocolate, featuring a range of uncommon bars, im-
ported boxed chocolates, and local specialty chocolates. Invariably, the chocolate department goes by a French name, such as
"Le Chocolatier" or "Au Chocolat" or "La Maison du Bonbon."

The reason for this recent proliferation of chocolate departments is that shrewd department store managers have come to realize that an unusual, high-quality chocolate section will "bring in traffic."

Wherever store management recognizes the importance of its chocolate department, you are assured of finding exquisite confectionery.

But you will probably pay through the snout for it.

SPECIALTY SHOPS

"Specialty Shops" is a catch-all term for small retailers of made-on-the-premises confectionery. These shops thrive mostly by offering fresh and unusual chocolate creations.

COIFFURES
EN
CHOCOLAT

In most cases, the solid chocolate products "made" by specialty shops are actually just molded by them from bulk chocolate ordered from a large manufacturer. The machinery for chocolate-making is very elaborate, and it would simply be impractical for a small shop to actually make its own chocolate.

MOM'S
CHOCOLATES

What specialty shops do genuinely make is *chocolates*: the unique fillings are created by the shop

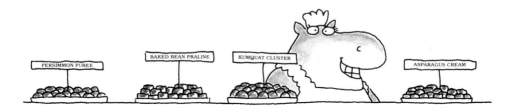

and they are then dipped by hand in the same wholesale chocolate that the shop uses for molding shapes.

There is a great mystique among chocolates connoisseurs about hand dipping—it seems to connote craftsmanship, care, and quality. But as with chocolate-processing machinery, coating equipment is complex and expensive, so a small chocolatier really has no choice but to coat chocolates by hand. Given this, it is possible to overestimate the intrinsic value of hand dipping.

DRUGSTORES

In an emergency, look for a drugstore. They are often open when other stores are closed, and they do sell over-the-counter chocolate.

Be aware, though, that since pharmacists have a virtual monopoly on off-hour chocolate, they tend to be somewhat blasé about freshness.

CHOCOLATE BY MAIL

If you have no ready access to fine chocolate, or if you simply want to become more well-rounded, you should try sending away for your chocolate. The only real disadvantage to mail-ordering is that your timing has to be near-perfect. The chocolate may arrive late

or you may arrive late

or a neighbor might arrive right on time.

CHOCOLATE INTERNATIONAL

When traveling abroad, the quickest and most reliable way to find chocolate is to ask around:

"Excuse me, where is the nearest chocolate?"

FRANCE, BELGIUM, SWITZERLAND

"Excusez-moi, où est le chocolat le plus proche?"

(Ex-COOZ-ay mwah, oo ay l'shō-cō-LAH l'ploo prōsh?)

GERMANY, AUSTRIA, SWITZERLAND

"Entschuldigen Sie bitte, wo ist die nächste Schokolade?"

(Ent-SHOOL-dee-gen 'zee BIT-tuh. vō ist dee NEX-tuh shō-cō-LAR-duh?)

RUSSIA

"ИЗВИНИТЕ, ГДЕ НАХОДИТСЯ БЛИЖАЙШИЙ ШОКОЛАД?"

(Eez-vee-NEE-tyuh, g-DYUH nock-CŌ-dee-tsah bleezh-i-SHEE shō-cō-LAHD?)

ANCIENT ROME

"Ardonpay emay, erewhay isyay ethay earestnay ocolatechay?"

(AR-dun-pay EE-may, AYR-way IZ-yay UH-thay EER-ist-nay OCK-lit-chay?)

ENGLAND

"I say, beg pardon, Old Man, but could you direct me to a nearby purveyor of chocolate, eh what?"

(AH-ee SEH-ee, behg PAH-dun, uhld mahn, baht cood ee-OO die-RECT mee too ay NEE-ah-BAH-ee puh-VAY-aw ruv CHUCK-uh-litt, ay hwuht?)

"THE SPIRIT OF JUST DESSERTS"

A PROUD FIGURE, BLINDFOLDED, MIXING UTENSIL
HELD ALOFT; BAR AND SCALES.

THE POLITICS OF CHOCOLATE

Nothing imparts such a potent sense of well-being as chocolate in abundance. Yet this feeling of plenty is far more precarious, far more illusory than most of us realize. A deliberate cut-off of our bean supply by the Cacao Producing and Exporting Countries would bring our nation to a grinding halt. Will it take an embargo for us to recognize our vulnerability to the whims of a few nations around the Equator? Or will we mobilize now to establish friendly relations with CPEC or, better yet, simply annex a few key areas of the Tropics?

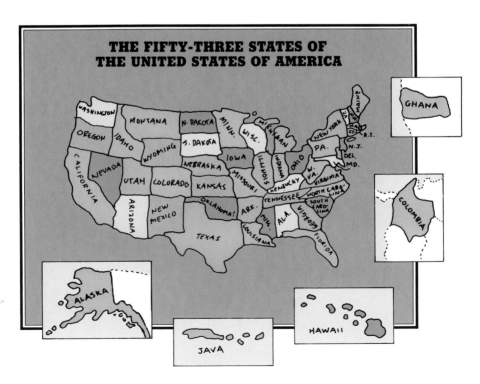

THE FIFTY-THREE STATES OF THE UNITED STATES OF AMERICA

And once we have protected our interests around the globe, we can turn our attention to home. There is growing discontent as many of our citizens feel that they are not getting a big enough slice of the pie.

If the current unequal distribution of chocolate continues unchecked, we increasingly run the risk of general depression.

Chocolate is not a privilege; it is a right. As such, it must be provided as a readily-available service in every state, in every community, on every block.

carbohydrant

TWO ENDS OF THE SPECTRUM

Individual of
Chocolate Sensibility

Individual of
Jellybean Sensibility

CREDITS